How Cowboy found his forever home

Gwen Keane

© Gwen Keane, November 2018.

All rights reserved. No part of this publication may be reproduced, distributed, or transmitted in any form or by any means, including photocopying, recording, or other electronic or mechanical methods, without the prior written permission of the publisher, except in the case of brief quotations embodied in critical reviews and certain other noncommercial uses permitted by copyright law.
For permission requests, write to the publisher, addressed "Attention: Permissions Coordinator," at the address below.

High Tide Publications, Inc.
1000 Bland Point Road
Deltaville, Virginia 23043
j.johansen@hightidepublications.com
www.hightidepublications.com

Ordering Information:

Available on Amazon.com, the publisher's website at www.hightidepublications.com, and from the *Northern Neck Partners for Pets* website at https://northernneckpartnersforpets.org
Quantity sales: Special discounts are available on quantity purchases by corporations, associations, and others. For details, contact the publisher at the address above.
Orders by U.S. trade bookstores and wholesalers: Ingram contact group is our distributor. (https://www.ingramcontent.com)

ISBN: 978-1-945990-24-3

All proceeds from this book are donated to *Northern Neck Partners for Pets*. Your donation will help build a private no-kill animal shelter, a safe haven for homeless and unwanted cats and dogs. Neither the author (Gwen Keane) or the publisher (High Tide Publications, Inc.) have received any compensation in the preparation or publishing of this book.

Cowboy

...the early years

My name is Cowboy. It wasn't always Cowboy. It was Dylan for a long time. How it got changed is what this story is about.

I am a beagle. I was born into a litter somewhere in the Northern Neck of Virginia. I grew up with other beagles and learned to hunt.

I am a hound. My nose is my guide through life. I am never happier than when I am following an interesting scent.

We hunted rabbits with our human when we got older. I lived in a pen with other beagles. We were outside no matter what the weather—hot, cold, rain, snow—you name it we saw it.

Beagles (if I do say so myself) are great dogs. But, because we are hounds, we can also be stubborn and require patient, creative training techniques.

I remember the last time I hunted with my pack. We were chasing a rabbit. I stepped into a hole, and hurt my leg.

No one picked me up. Instead, when my human saw I could not keep up with the other dogs, he went on and left me behind.

I thought he would come back when they had finished their run.

He didn't.

I hung around the spot for a couple of days. I really thought he would come for me.

Finally, I gave up. Hungry and injured, I tried to walk and hunt for food. I found a trash can with garbage and some food scraps.

The pickings were slim.

One morning, as I was walking down a road, I heard a truck. It stopped behind me, and I heard the door open and then footsteps. I wanted to run, but I couldn't. My leg hurt really bad, and I was weak from not eating.

A man walked around and looked down at me. I sat and he picked me up and carried me back to the truck. We drove to a big building. I heard a lot of dogs barking.

I was scared.

He carried me inside and talked to the woman at the desk. "I found another one," he said.

Another human came and got me. Then they put me in a big cage by myself and fed me. I ate and ate and ate. They named me Dylan.

It was very noisy in this big building. I learned it was the county shelter, and everyone there was very kind to me. I slept on a blanket, and every day someone came to clean my kennel and feed me.

One thing I noticed was dogs would be taken from their kennels and walk past me. They looked so sad.

They never came back.

Just as I was getting used to being full of food and clean, I saw two people coming toward my kennel...a man and a woman. The woman knelt down in front of the door to my kennel and started talking to me. "You are such a sweet dog, Dylan. I am going to take you with me to a doctor. We're going to see if we can get you adopted into a forever home."

"Forever home," I thought. "Whew! I am not going to that place the other dogs went. You know, where they never come back from."

We went to the animal doctor. She stayed with me the entire time. They stuck a needle in me. "Heart-worm positive," the doctor said.

"It's okay," the woman who brought me answered. "We'll pay for the treatment."

Then we left again. "Don't worry, Dylan. You'll be fine."

This time we went to another place. It smelled a lot better. There were dogs there, but it was quieter. The kennels were nicer too.

They gave me a bath and did something about my tick bites (which itched like crazy). The humans there took me out several times a day to play in the yard with balls and toys. They petted me and I felt safe.

But somehow I knew this was not my forever home.

Gwen
...the phone call

The call no animal lover wants—especially with two dogs and family obligations. But it came anyway!

"Gwen, we have a beagle and were wondering if..."

"The last thing I need is another dog."

"It's a foster situation until we can find him a home. His name is Dylan, a 4 year old beagle. He has a long way to go before he can be adopted. Being treated for heart worm and will have to be neutered. Very sweet little guy."

I looked over at Treme and Carter Lee. The cats were ignoring me.

Treme is my black lab and Carter Lee is a dapple mini-dachshund. The cats are Igor, Little Lulu, and Hugs.

"No, really. Please. Is there someone else you can call?"

Silence on the other end. I knew the answer.

"There are more animals than homes. The kill shelter is usually where they wind up. Heartbreaking, but hopefully when we get this new shelter built, it will make a difference."

"I'll come and take a look at him this afternoon. No commitment."

"Okay. Thanks."

It was May, and the first day Treme and Carter Lee had been able to be out on the screened porch. I left them at home, and drove to the kennel where Dylan was being boarded.

He was a beagle, and seemed to be recovering from his ordeal. "He hurt his leg. I think that is why he was abandoned," the attendant at the kennel said.

He looked up at me. I tried to not look back.

"He is on heart-worm treatment and needs to be neutered."

"Yes, I understand." I was unable to turn away from those brown eyes.

"He's not house broken."

"Is there anything else?"

"No, not really. Oh, he limps. We think he was out there alone in the world for some period of time, trying to survive."

I looked into those sorrowful eyes and wondered what life had been like for Dylan. He never stopped looking at me. In spite of all the adversity he had faced, he was a very sweet and loving dog.

"Okay, I'll foster him. But FOSTER is the key word."

House breaking a hound can be a challenge. But, those eyes!

So, off we went. He went with me willingly and seemed pretty relaxed.

"Let's go meet Treme and Carter Lee!"

Cowboy

...Treme and Carter Lee

This woman kept staring at me. I tried to look away, but she kept watching me.

She took me out to her car. There was a little animal bed in the front seat. She was so gentle when she picked me up and put me on the seat next to her. I did not move or make a sound. I was scared, but she kept talking to me.

"It's okay, Dylan. You'll be fine."

She had a nice voice.

We got to our destination, and she came around and lifted me out of the car. She walked me around so I could do my business. So many new smells! My nose was sure busy.

We went inside, and there were two other dogs!

The big, black one (a Labrador retriever named Treme) was really friendly. She walked right over to me.

The other one (a little dapple dachshund named Carter Lee) looked shocked to see me. I guess the nice lady didn't get her permission.

Later I would learn there were three cats in the house. One was named Igor. He was a white cat, and really nice.

The second cat was Little Lulu. She rested high up on a shelf and looked down at me. I think I needed her permission to stay there.

It must have been her house.

I heard a noise and looked up. Not another cat! I found out her name was Hugs. She was a calico and she was always getting into things.

I had some lunch.

Then the lady (who I found out was named Gwen) dumped a bunch of strange looking things onto the floor in front of me.

I chose a bone, and gnawed on it for awhile. Then I fell asleep.

After awhile, I woke up. Treme was next to me on the floor. I know we will be good friends. I can tell.

When it got dark, Gwen put a comfortable bed by her big bed and put me on it. I fell asleep, waking myself up a couple of times because I was snoring. We did this every night.

Is this my forever home?

Gwen

...One Day at a Time

After a couple of days, I noticed Igor was sleeping next to Dylan. Treme lay close by. Carter Lee was leery, and Little Lulu and Hugs ignored him totally.

We went through the house training exercise, his daily heart worm treatment, and acclimating him to living inside a house.

I started looking for a forever home for him. After all, I had agreed to do this temporarily. I was only providing a temporary home for Dylan prior to adoption.

Meanwhile, Dylan had really settled in to our daily routine.

Treme loved the sun, and tried to get Dylan to join her. But Dylan did not like the sun and preferred to sniff around the yard or to nap inside.

At first he just curled up on a rug.

Later he discovered other comfortable places to nap.

But his favorite place was to lay beside Treme on her bed.

However, he never turned down an opportunity to take an afternoon snooze with Igor.

Sometimes it seemed that Dylan recalled the days when he was homeless. He would get a sad look in his eyes. It was then he would seek comfort from Treme.

Treme is a certi ied therapy dog. Not only does she visit schools and retirement homes, but she also serves as our personal family therapist.

(Papa Olav and Treme as a pup getting ready to go for a walk at Hughlett Point.)

    Our family has always opened our home and hearts to animals in need. Many year ago, I rescued a six-week-old puppy and named him Olav. When Treme joined our family, he was given the name Papa Olav. For ten years, Treme learned a lot from Papa Olav.

When Treme was a pup, Olav would smile after discovering Santa had left toys. He willingly shared the toys with Treme, living up to his name Papa Olav.

On Treme's first Christmas, she received a huge teddy bear. At the end of a very exciting day, she fell asleep next to her Teddy.

When Carter Lee (our mini-dachsund) was brought home as a pup, Treme became her nanny.

Carter Lee is now grown. I could see she was nurturing Dylan just as Treme had nurtured her and made her feel welcome.

Cowboy
...Frosting on My Nose

I never lived inside a house before. I had to learn to let the humans know when I had to go to the bathroom. That way they could let me out.

At first, I had a few accidents. But, after awhile I got the hang of it, thanks to Treme.

We have parties here. They call them birthday parties, and everyone gets a treat.

The first one I ever went to was for Treme. Treme celebrated her sixth birthday in July, 2018.

At Treme's party, they told me it was okay to accept the cupcake.

And after the excitement, I rested next to Treme, licking the icing from my nose.

One day, I was resting on one of the dog beds. Carter Lee came over and cuddled up next to me. After that, she was my buddy forever.

Gwen was watching from the doorway.

From that day on, she called me Cowboy. She said it was impossible to let me go. That was the day I found my forever home.

Oh, and I stopped calling her Gwen.

Now I call her mom.

About the Author

Gwen Keane was born and raised in the Northern Neck of Virginia. She holds a Bachelor of Arts in Business Administration from Trinity University in Washington, D.C. and graduated cum laude from Georgetown University where she received a Master of Public Administration.

She grew up with animals, including wildlife, and learned from her grandmother to always help animals in need.

Being an animal lover Gwen participates in dog activities. She has been an active member of the Northern Neck Kennel Club since 2003.

Gwen serves on the board of the Northern Neck Partners for Pets (NNPP). All profits from the sale of this book will be donated to NNPP.

Saving Unwanted Cats and Dogs

Northern Neck Partners for Pets provides a safe haven for homeless pets.

Who We Are

Lancova Partners for Pets, doing business as Northern Neck Partners for Pets (NNPP), is an advocate for the compassionate treatment of unwanted animals. Organized in 2014 by concerned citizens and incorporated as a 501(c)(3), our mission is to provide humane care, treatment, and adoption services for homeless pets.

With your help, we can achieve our goal to build the Northern Neck's first private no-kill shelter.

NNPP is a grassroots, all-volunteer nonprofit whose vision is to end animal cruelty and foster a community where pets can live without fear, hunger, or needless pain and suffering.

Our only focus is to help homeless and unwanted pets by providing a safe and secure haven until they find forever homes. Privately funded and operated, this shelter will strive to find quality homes for all healthy and treatable dogs and cats. And not cost the county a dime.

NNPP believes that euthanasia should be used only in cases when it advances the word's true meaning: a merciful end. And we pledge not to kill healthy, adoptable, or treatable animals.

This initiative places NNPP in a leadership role for humane and compassionate rescue: the Virginia Federation of Humane Societies launched "Save VA Pets – Crossing the No-Kill Finish Line" program this year. This statewide No-Kill effort aims to reduce the death rate to 10% by 2020 and then continue until all adoptable and treatable animals are saved.

If you are inspired by the No-Kill movement, please help us end needless euthanasia.

Providing a Safe Haven for Homeless Pets

Across the country, overburdened shelters take in millions of stray, abused, and lost animals every year and struggle to find safe, loving homes for them.

And it is no different here.

Despite the valiant efforts of Northern Neck animal control staff, county shelters in Lancaster, Northumberland, and Westmoreland/Richmond have one of the highest euthanasia rates in the Commonwealth.

Why is this happening? Simply put, animal welfare is a low funding priority for county government.

Studies demonstrate that rural shelters struggle to keep up the influx of unwanted and homeless animals. Not enough room. Not enough money. Not enough adoptions.

What causes the demand? Animals allowed to roam, pets that are not spayed or neutered, lost hunting dogs, neglected and abused animals, and abandoned pets. Virginia 2016 statistics show that 1,090 cats and dogs were taken into Northern Neck public shelters.

30 to 40% of these were euthanized after the state-mandated waiting periods. Five days for pets without tags; ten for those with tags.

The heart-breaking part is that many of these helpless animals were healthy and well-behaved. They could have been beloved family pets.

NNPP salutes the work of our county animal control staff who work tirelessly to save adoptable dogs and cats by partnering with local and regional rescues. Some fortunate at-risk animals are transferred to other states and no-kill facilities where there is a strong demand for healthy and happy companions. Some are placed in foster homes. Too many are euthanized.

The sad fact is that approximately 300 plus cats and dogs die each year in our local shelters.

The bottom line is that there is simply no public funding for the long-term care, nurturing, training, and marketing that would significantly reduce deaths and increase adoptions.

Thus, it falls to the nonprofit sector to supply these essential services.

If saving vulnerable animals in the Northern Neck resonates with you, please help us raise the funds needed to build a no-kill shelter.

Thanks!

Cowboy

www.ingramcontent.com/pod-product-compliance
Lightning Source LLC
Chambersburg PA
CBHW060856090426
42736CB00025B/3497